THE PROCESS OF FORGIVENESS

THE EFFECT IN MARRIAGE

THOMAS & NATASHA GIBSON

DIVINE FLOW PUBLISHING, LTD

THE PROCESS OF FORGIVENESS

THE EFFECT IN MARRIAGE

And the two shall become one
Walking together in agreement
Commanding the blessings of the Lord

As One Ministry

Empowering couples with tools for a successful marriage.

May you always
have a heart to
give + recieve forgivness!
Much love,
Thomas + Natasha

Library of Congress Catalog Number: 2021900636

ISBN: 978-1-7364267-0-8

Published by As One Ministry, USA

Cover design and layout by Divine Flow Publishing, Ltd.

Author's Photo credit: J. Chatmon

Printed in the United States of America

TESTIMONIALS

"Just want to thank the two of you for helping my family in a time of need. Your meticulous guidance and expertise has been very useful and instrumental in how my wife and I approach obstacles in our relationship."

~ B. & J. T.

"We were blessed to find both Thomas and Tasha at the time that we did in our marriage. God has a way of placing the right people in your life at the right time. Thank you for helping us re-identify God in our marriage and in our lives. Blessings always."

~ J. & C. W.

"Good morning. Thank you all very much for a great time last night. God truly has some strong soldiers working for him! May you all continue to be blessed by the Best!"

~ J. & D. B.

"Thomas & Tasha, thank you for being there for me during the hardest time of my marriage and helping us strengthen each other to bring a life into this world. Love you!"

~ M. & C. W.

"Thank you so much for extending your time and hospitality to us on Sunday. Your coaching put in perspective how we should forgive, ask questions then with a pure heart forgive and give it to God so true healing can begin. I am so thankful for the tools you have provided to us and have faith that God will restore lost trust. You both are an inspiration to our marriage! Thank you so much again for helping us!"

~ **Z. & K. L.**

"Natasha, I just wanted to let you know how much I appreciate what you and Thomas do for marriages. I did not appreciate what you all offered until my husband and I met with our marriage counselor at our church. The difference I noticed immediately was when we left our session with you all, my husband and I were holding hands and were encouraged to talk things through using the tools that was given to us. When we left our church marriage counselor, we not only weren't holding hands, but we were also encouraged to not talk about what we had just spent the last hour talking about! We'd like to schedule another session soon with you and Thomas soon!"

~ **D. & D. W.**

"Thank you so much for investing in us. The coaching and practical skills you taught us transformed our marriage. You guys are truly remarkable life coaches. We are truly blessed to have you in our lives!"

~ **S. & S. R.**

FOREWORD

I remember the first time I met Thomas. I was leading a men's intensive retreat that Thomas was attending. I witnessed Thomas' willingness to allow God to change whatever He desired in Thomas' life. His passion to be a sold-out Christ follower was inspiring.

I was so impressed with Thomas that I sought him out and asked him if he would be willing to serve with me on subsequent events. His yes led him over the next three years to travel the country with me and serve as my right-hand man on over 30 retreats. During those retreats, I saw how Thomas faithfully called Natasha every night before bed, connecting with her heart as a loving and attentive husband.

The Process of Forgiveness was written from Thomas & Natasha's own experiences of loss, betrayal, divorce, but ultimately of love, redemption, restoration, and forgiveness as they applied God's word and worked through their issues. They've 'walked the talk' of this book and it is their greatest desire to see God work in others' marriages as they experience The Process of Forgiveness.

As a men's pastor at a mega-sized church and having led freedom ministry events for over 18 years, I often get asked to counsel couples going through marital issues. Thomas and Natasha are my go-to couple to send couples needing marriage coaching. Over the years I can honestly say that 100% of the couples that embrace and implement the biblical truths shared in The Process of Forgiveness have had their marriages restored and are now flourishing.

I am grateful for God's anointing on Thomas and Natasha to lead couples to a place many only dream about and that is two becoming one. I'm also excited that you can have the marriage God desires and that you deserve as you begin The Process of Forgiveness.

Paul Panquerne
Men's Ministry
Covenant Church

DEDICATION

In Loving Memory of our grandparents.
Without you paving the way for our parents, we would not be here to do the things God has called us to do. It is an honor and a privilege to be a part of your lineage.

Thank you for your personal sacrifices you made known and unknown. We pray we have made you proud and know we are proud to honor you with our first publication and it is only fitting that your names are printed as well.

Robert Lee and Annie Laura Babbles.
The grandad and grandmother who ensured all of your children and grandchildren had a good spiritual foundation.
It was a pleasure to sit in the garden behind the garage and eat fresh vegetables and fruit with the woman who would motivate me while I served in the Army in Europe.
I am grateful to grandad for teaching me the secret marinade sauce that I still use to this day.

To Lindsey Gibson my biological grandad and name-sake who I got to meet in the latter years of your life.

Grandad and Grandma Edward and Mae Taylor, thank you for the wonderful memories we shared together. Grandad, I'll always remember the laughter we shared and how I always looked forward to coming to see you. Grandma, I'll always remember your soft and silent demeanor that was so powerful in every way. I'll always be your "Totsie".

Grandma Hattie Snipes, thank you for helping to raise me and instilling in me the strength to endure whatever life brings my way. The wonderful memories of watching you make your homemade biscuits warms my heart this day. I am so honored to be called Ms. Hattie's granddaughter!

We wish you were here to see our families today, but we know you have the best view ever and we look forward to being with you again!

Much love always!

ACKNOWLEDGMENTS

"Behold, I will do a new thing; now it shall spring forth; shall ye not know it? I will even make a way in the wilderness, and rivers in the desert." ~ Isaiah 43:19

This book is made possible only through the one who created us. The term, *"What God has created, let no man put asunder"* will forever ring true in our hearts. The purpose of writing this guide is to help heal marriages and we are only able to write it because we reflected on one of our personal and greatest challenges in marriage; The Process of Forgiveness.

We are so grateful to our heavenly Father, for His grace and mercy that renews every day, our Lord and Savior, Jesus Christ for the shedding of His blood and for reconciling us back to the Father, and Holy Spirit for teaching us the ways of the Father and birthing this process through us!

Thanks to our parents, Manuel Taylor, Janice Anderson, Thomas Sneed, and Minnie Bladen through whom God selected to introduce us to this world to have our life experiences and testimony.

Pastor Freddie Moore, who married us twice.

Pastors Calvin and Linda Watson for their friendship, support, and trust. Thank you for being obedient to God's leading in developing us for our ministry licenses. We will forever be grateful for your faith in us.

We would also like to acknowledge our three children, Raven, Roman, and Rolando Gibson whom we are very proud of and for whom we continue to pray for daily. Our two handsome grandsons, Shamaar and Levi Gibson who we have pronounced to be a warrior and priest for the Kingdom of God here on earth. We dearly love each of you.

A special thanks to Shane and Shelia Pitcock, who sowed the first seed into making this publication a reality. Freda Dents for helping with the initial edit of this book. The countless clients who have trusted us with the implementation of "The Process of Forgiveness" into their marriages.

Kym Panquerne for continued prayers, ministry mentoring, and behind the scene support.

Camelle and Team at Divine Flow Publishing for all of their hardwork and long hours in making this vision a reality.

We "give a shout out" to the prayer warriors who participate in our weekly virtual meetings for women through Wives of Power and for men through Kingdom Husbands. Thank you for your continuous prayers in support of As One Ministry.

We would be remiss if we did not acknowledge our family and friends who are too numerous to name individually, across this country and around the world. May Papa bless you all with the desires of your heart and may he continue to grant you a life of prosperity; mentally, physically, socially, spiritually, and financially. In Jesus' name! Amen! Amen! And, Amen!

Thank you for loving us through it all! We love every one of you.

TABLE OF CONTENTS

INTRODUCTION

Imagine a wall that is made of many bricks and you desire to get to the other side of that wall. You only have two tools, a chisel, and a hammer. How would you approach this situation? You would dismantle the wall by removing one brick at a time. The same goes for resolving marital conflict. Every issue in your marriage is a representation of a brick in the wall which has been built between you and your spouse. During the process of conflict resolution, you have to focus on one conflict or 'brick' at a time.

Through our story, we hope to show you how it's possible to pull down your walls and build the successful marriage you both dreamed of.

Although many truths are in the Bible, some are not revealed until God allows them according to his timing. We Christians refer to such knowledge and understanding as a Rhema word. It's not until we were divorced from one another and were reunited and remarried, did we recognize, "The Process of Forgiveness;" thus our Rhema word. It was then that we realized God had done something unique in us and wanted to complete a work of reconciliation, restoration, and healing through the process of forgiveness.

We would be remised if we said that the process has worked for everyone. However, what we can say is that if both persons are willing to trust the word of God and not their feelings, it has been proven to work 100% of the time. "***So shall my word be that goeth forth out of my mouth: it shall not return unto me void, but it shall accomplish that which I please, and it shall prosper in the thing whereto I sent it." ~ Isaiah 55:11***

We often have the opportunity to share our marital testimony with the hope that it will touch someone's heart and move them into true repentance and forgiveness. We hope our testimony brings revelation knowledge and that it doesn't matter why we fall but how and why we get back up. We have learned in our falling, to get up with the intent to not fall for the same reason. No one enters marriage with dreams of walking down the aisle of matrimony together only to experience walking up the steps of a courthouse headed towards divorce, yet according to the 2019 American Community Survey*, 14.9 divorces out of 1,000 marriages occur. We were, sadly, caught up in this cycle after only eight years of marriage.

All marriages experience ups and downs. Consider the waves of an ocean at the beach. When the water is calm you experience a steady rise and fall of the waves that allow you to swim without a struggle. However, when the waves are high and rough, it is difficult to keep swimming with the current and it's usually a sign that a storm is near. When a storm is brewing you quickly become exhausted and want to quit. It's the same with marriage. You want the steady, consistent waves to help build stamina and strengthen your love, patience, kindness, and other spiritual muscles that are likened to the fruit of the Spirit (Galatians 5:22). Experiencing a marriage that has extreme ups and downs is not ideal, and signals a major storm is brewing.

Fear not, because achieving great balance in marriage is possible with the right tools and Godly communication. There is a specific scripture in the Bible that asks a great question. ***"Can two walk together, except they be agreed?" ~ Amos 3:3*** It is a known fact that people with individual desires and expectations will experience hurts and pains caused by themselves and their spouses. And the greatest known catalyst to peace in marital communication, at this time, is the process of forgiveness.

What we have discovered in our marital relationship is that forgiveness is not comprised of words alone but a pattern that, when followed, brings about reconciliation, healing, restoration, and freedom. Every conflict in marriage is unique to the individuals experiencing them and each conflict can be resolved through a pattern designed for each couple.

Take for example one of our clients who were referred to us for marriage coaching. When they walked through the door, we could sense the tension between them. We began with introductions and prayer, then asked why they came to see us. They shared their story and we shared ours. The wife stated that this meeting was her last-ditch effort to make the marriage work. They had experienced counseling before and were only with us because they were referred by a mutual friend. After two hours of implementing the process of forgiveness, they left the house holding hands and were very appreciative of each other. Because of the work God had done in them they were able to hear each other's hearts and let down their guards for the first time in their marriage.

Our desire is not for couples to continue to see us for marriage coaching for months or years on end. We want them to learn to implement the tools we share so they can be empowered to have a successful marriage. Ultimately, they will use the same processes and tools to make disciples through their marital lifestyle.

We are not licensed counselors so we do not diagnose mental, sociological, or psychological issues, but we do believe this book can help you overcome life's and marriage's most difficult hurdles. It's designed to be used as a tool of reference and an instructional guide from chapter to chapter. It's a practical tool that gets results in real situations whether you are married or not. Know that the process of forgiveness can be learned and implemented in any relationship (parent/child, friendship, workplace, and many more).

We intentionally created this book to be short and direct to allow for the process of healing to take place optimally for the two people using its instruction and pattern. We also recommend going through the worksheets at the end of this book to help you go deeper within each step of the process.

You will find in the first part of this book, we take you through our story from the perspective of "His side" and "Her side". By doing this, we hope that you'll be able to connect the story along with the process in the book for greater impact.

Now, let's get to it!

PART I

HOW WE GOT HERE

OUR TESTIMONY

HER SIDE AND HIS SIDE

Her Side:

August 1999 the divorce became final and I was faced with "what next?" I was ready for a change as it had been a full year since the separation, and I'd spoken to my then ex-husband only twice, and one was the night before the divorce was final. Sure, I had thought about the future, but it was not until this moment, the thought of leaving my home state of North Carolina came to me.

It was like God didn't release this part of the plan for my life until that very moment. I recall telling my mom I was moving to Texas. Her immediate response was "can't you move to Charlotte?" Gotta love moms, right? I said, if I'm going to leave, I'm going to go big. After all, if it didn't work out, it wasn't like I couldn't come back. But deep down, I knew that was not an option for me. Once I get my mind set on something, I literally get tunnel vision or in my case blind to other options. As you will read later, having this characteristic can bite you when it's unhealthy.

You see, at the age of 14, I became relationally involved with a 17-year-old teenager from my neighborhood. The relationship wasn't favored by my mother or my grandmother of whom we (me, my mom, and brothers) were living with at the time; and it was always rocky. What I didn't know at that time was that this pattern of breaking up and getting back together would continue for the next 25 years of my life.

So, in relocating to Texas, the last thing on my radar was being in another relationship and quite frankly, I just wanted to experience life as a single woman with no ties. Sounded pretty refreshing to me but I wasn't totally relationship-free.

His Side:

I confessed Jesus Christ as my Lord and Savior at age eleven. Between that time and meeting Natasha, I did what many people do – strayed away from God and began living a secular lifestyle. I was previously married for seven years and had three children with my first wife. We were divorced in 1997 and I continued life living secularly with a knowledge of Jesus Christ without a relationship with Him.

After dating for a few years and experiencing the hurt that can be caused by a lack of full commitment to Christ, I decided to focus on establishing a life that would draw me closer to God.

Several months before I met Natasha, I made a vow to God that I would not seek a mate. I told Him that I would wait on Him to bring me the woman He wanted me to have. In the following months, I focused on my job and spent time with my children when I had custody of them. I began to read the Bible and seek the answers to a lot of questions I had.

Her Side:

I met Thomas as a work colleague in March 2000. We worked together on a couple of projects and ultimately in December 2000, I asked him if he was interested in accompanying me to the company holiday event. He accepted only if I would have lunch with him before the event. I accepted the lunch invitation, and we were inseparable from that point.

I recall during our second date, I heard in my spirit, "this is your husband" and I remembered saying to God "Really? I'm not even looking" and I just brushed it off.

As we dated, we called that our 'interview' time, we really got to know one another. Thomas proposed to me in late February 2001 and we were married on August 25, 2001. Interesting fact, we delayed our honeymoon till one week after the wedding and literally returned from Mexico one day before the unfortunate events of 9/11. I am so thankful that God's favor was upon us, as truly I couldn't imagine being stranded in another country while that kind of turmoil was going on in the United States.

Keeping things moving as I'm known to do, we set out our goals as husband and wife and a blended family. We established, early on, boundaries for our marriage and family and the kids became 'our' kids from that point. I thought it was important to share with the kids that I was not taking their biological mother's place and I expected them to always respect her as I intended to do the same. So, our kids never felt pressured to have a forced relationship but one of mutual respect.

His Side:

The first time I noticed Natasha was on an elevator at work and I thought to myself, 'she's fine.' The one thing that stopped me from approaching her was the ring on her finger. Having experienced an unfaithful marriage, I determined I would not be the one to spoil another person's marriage. So, I said, "hello" to her and she responded in kind, and when the doors of the elevator opened, she quickly ran out (now remember, this is my side of the story regardless of what she says).

Surprisingly, Natasha called me on my desk phone at work and asked me out on a date for the company Christmas party. I recalled asking her about the ring on her finger and she assured me that she was not married. I asked her for her cell phone number so that I could call her later. After the call I prayed to God while sitting at my desk, asking if this was the woman He had for me. I got no immediate answer that I could recognize and finished the day's work.

When I arrived home that evening, I called Tasha and made arrangements to have a date before the Christmas party to ensure that we would be compatible at the four hour-long event. We had dinner, went to see a movie, and I made every effort to be a gentleman the entire evening. We talked about quite a few things that evening during dinner; children, former marriages, family, friends, favorite colors, likes, and dislikes. It was more of an interview session than anything else. I was shocked when during the movie, she kissed me! Of course, I reciprocated, and we went for a midnight walk around a local Dallas lake to top off the evening.

After a few months of dating, I invited Natasha over for dinner one evening and we played Scrabble afterward. At the end of the evening I spelled out a question to her on the board and when she read the message, she screamed, "Yes! Yes! Yes!" What I had spelled out on the Scrabble board was, "Will you marry me?" Eight months later we were married.

One thing we agreed to was not to belittle one another and to always work at getting past our problems. I was growing in my relationship with God and with her. Later, an opportunity arose for us to have custody of the children and she asked what I wanted to do. My reply was, I wanted to fight for my kids. We were granted custody and Tasha embraced the children as though they were her own.

It was a few years later things started to go south for me. Intimacy was on the decline. Conversations about how to improve that area of our lives and efforts to do so were often rejected. The one positive in our lives was we raised the children to achieve goals, love God, and respect adults. We witnessed the baptism of our two sons, our daughter had already been baptized, and financially we were stable and able to be a blessing to others.

My relationship with God was flourishing to the point that I had been given my purpose in life and moved forward in that direction. What bothered me was why I could not get the support of my wife where the ministry was concerned. Things took a turn for the worst when I asked her if she was in love with me and her answer was, "No." That took a lot out of me. Here was the woman of my dreams, so dedicated to work, the children, friends, and service to others, yet I had to take a back seat.

Her side:

After 7 years of marriage to Thomas, things were good as you've read on Thomas' side, these were the years of collecting stuff and doing a lot. Building a family, working crazy hours, commuting two hours one way just to get to work (thank God we both loved our jobs), volunteering at church in every free moment we had, we did A LOT except for the most important thing. I'm just truly thankful to God that He wastes nothing!

I remember the moment it all changed for me. I was on my way home from work one evening and received the text 'Hey lady, how are you?' If I'd known what my next step would take me through, I would have probably thrown the phone out of the window and ran for the hills. (Oh, wait! That's what I did when I relocated to Texas! You see, not only was I ready to leave my home state, but I was also running to get away from the biggest stronghold of my life!)

Although Thomas and I thoroughly interviewed each other during our dating months, he failed to ask "what baggage I would be bringing into the relationship?" And I failed to fully disclose the baggage I would be bringing into the relationship. As I stated earlier, I became involved in a serious relationship at an early age, which often led to baby mama drama, break ups... get back togethers and of course I was always being untruthful to my mom and grandmother of my whereabouts for the first two years of the relationship. Shortly after I graduated from high school, I called off the relationship altogether. I met my first husband a while afterward but during that marriage, I somehow managed to get back involved with the ex-boyfriend. Eventually, it turned out that my first husband and I were both being unfaithful to one another and this led to my first divorce, and my relocation to Texas, now you know the full story.

Although there was no sexual contact with the ex-boyfriend, there were still occasional phone calls during my marriage to Thomas. I have learned that there doesn't have to be physical contact to commit adultery as ***Matthew 5:28 states: But I say unto you, that whosoever looketh on a woman to lust after her hath committed adultery with her already in his heart.***

Eventually, this would cause me to be unsettled at the drop of a hat and of course would cause unnecessary tension between Thomas and me. It all came out and Thomas knew of the ex-boyfriend and this was when major problems started between us. I didn't have a support system where I felt I could be transparent and walk this out without having someone in my business or passing judgment on me. I was attending church, operating in a leadership capacity, knew the word but didn't see anything wrong with keeping a friendship with the ex-boyfriend. I didn't want to cause shame on myself or make anything big out of nothing and I certainly didn't want to bring any unwanted shame down on Thomas.

Our marriage became more like roommates. There was a lack of intimacy, communication was very minimal. On the outside, we were the perfect couple, but behind closed doors, it was a total joke. I believed the lie of the enemy and that was "life is too short to be miserable" and I needed to take action to fix it. It led me to do what I knew best and what was familiar to me and that was to get away from the situation... run! But I didn't realize that God had another plan for me. I divorced Thomas with the intention of not wanting to hurt him anymore by dealing with this issue head-on.

His side:

I often wondered what I had done wrong to make Tasha suddenly lose interest in me. I questioned whether the weight that I had gained was the issue and she would tell me, "No." I then began to look introspectively and question my manhood. Was I a provider, did I drink too much, had I said or done something wrong? Each time I asked her about these characteristics she would say, "No."

It was not until the death of Tasha's grandmother that I realized the problem. As we stood at the gravesite after the burial service, I was speaking with one of her relatives and noticed Tasha speaking to someone I had not met. As I approached the conversation stopped and Tasha introduced me to the man she was speaking with. I asked who he was and what he did but the conversation died out after that. I thought to myself, another person who does not communicate well. It made me feel a little uneasy, but I thought nothing of it.

Later that day, we were at Tasha's uncle's home and her cell phone was ringing inside her purse. I looked at the number and it was the name of a female that I did not know. I let it roll into voicemail and thought about checking it. Doing so would have been out of the norm for me so I didn't.

About an hour later that name popped into my mind and I pressed past my desire not to check her phone and I listened to her voicemail. Turns out the female name was cover for the man I met at the gravesite and in the message was an invitation for the two of them to meet before we left town. When I confronted Tasha about this, she was irate at me for checking her voicemail. It was at that moment that I understood the disconnect in our relationship. I called the man from the graveyard and told him to discontinue conversation with my wife because he was causing conflict in our marriage. He tried to convince me they were just friends. The conversation ended cordially but that did not change anything in my marriage to Tasha.

A few months later Tasha asked me for a time of separation. I told her that she had no cause to leave and that she needed to fix the situation. A few days later she decided to pack her bags and I let her know that there was no biblical cause for her actions, and that if she left the house, I wanted a divorce. She left and I prayed to God, asking Him why she would not listen to me. His response was, "If she will not listen to me, what makes you think she is going to listen to you?"

I thanked God that I had the relationship with Him that I did. The fleshly side of me wanted to go out and find the closest bar and drink my sorrows away. But God was not finished with me. After I walked around the house, mad at the world and my wife, I heard a voice in my head and heart; He said, "Thomas, I am with you. I want you to be patient because she will be back." My immediate response was. 'She should've never left.' I received the divorce papers from Natasha and explained to our sons what happened and why Natasha was not home anymore. We met at the courthouse, finalized the documents, and parted ways. I was angry, disgusted, frustrated, and still in love with her. I had no male accountability partner at the time to talk to about what I was going through, and I sank into a state of confusion about why this was happening. I knew I could hear the voice of God, but all I was getting was a message to stay focused on Him and to continue with life as it was.

Her side:

Shortly after the divorce, I reached out to the ex-boyfriend, but things quickly started going downhill and I was more confused than ever. I then realized how God was starting to strip away the lies and despite the mess, I was creating for myself, God was faithful and protective. After a few months, I knew I had to end the relationship but after 25 years of believing my truth, this was hard to accept.

I began attending church on a regular basis again, quite honestly, I didn't have anyone I could confide in. I felt ashamed, embarrassed, and I remembered being mad at myself, but I knew I was tired of running and living a lie. I had always said I didn't want to be a hypocrite. I knew I wasn't perfect, I didn't want to intentionally lead a double life. I knew my life was not pleasing God. Too many people had been hurt over the years and I needed to take ownership of that.

I joined a Search for Significance Women's group and that's when my breakthrough continued. As I was going through the class, I remember these three words came to me **"Restored, Redeemed, and Liberty."** God had me do two distinctive things that He knew would bring me complete healing and without a doubt, I would receive and know that I was taking the steps towards true healing.

I remember the evening God confirmed what I needed to do to begin bringing closure to this part of my life. I needed to put it in writing as well as verbalize it. So, I called the ex-boyfriend and the conversation did not go well at all. After the phone call, I began to write.

I started writing a letter to my two then ex-husbands and the ex-boyfriend asking for their forgiveness. After completing the letters, I sent them via snail mail (USPS), so there was no recall or delete buttons... they were on the way. When I sent the letters, I knew this was the end. The scripture, ***"You shall know the truth and the truth shall make you free" ~ John 8:32*** made me realize that I had accepted and had been living a lie and now I was not only seeing truth but walking in it. This scripture has been my anthem ever since because I was finally free, and little did I know the work was just beginning.

Also, I did not connect the dots at that time, but I had applied God's number one principle: Confess your sins one to another. I asked God for His forgiveness, received it, and was ready to move on, without baggage, for the first time in 25 years!

I then began to write a list of characteristics I was looking for in my next husband and when I finished writing them, I heard God say, "You have that." Not being married, this brought about a puzzled look and then Thomas' name came into my spirit.

A few days later, I would find myself contacting Thomas regarding a health issue. Little did I know, he would call later to follow up and ask how I was feeling. Eventually, we would have additional conversations, which led me to inquire about the letter and asking him for his forgiveness again.

His side:

The reality was, I could not do a thing about the situation, so I moved on. I spent time with the boys, kept in touch with my daughter, and visited my mother more often than I usually would. The next time I saw Tasha would be a few months later at my son's high school football game. I was there with a female I was dating and that was the last place I expected to see her. I introduced them and went on with life... (in my mind).

It was a few days later that I got a phone call from Tasha asking if we could talk. I said "yes" and we met, and she asked for my forgiveness, apologized, and explained to me what had happened to her over the past months. I forgave her and later prayed to God about what I had heard, and He said, "I told you she would be back."

Her side:

One year to the date that I left, we began dating again. Later that year in August, on what would have been our 9th Wedding Anniversary, we wedded again with our same Pastor of whom we also asked his forgiveness.

Our relationship had been restored, our marriage redeemed, and I was truly free!

I believe my testimony is for people who are hurting because of the stronghold of past relationships and spiritual soul ties. It is keeping them bound and living a life of lies. To my amazement, when I'm led to share my testimony with other women, some share they are dealing with the same issue of a past relationship and don't know how to overcome it.

We become so involved in relationships at an early age, that we don't give ourselves time to know God and know how a godly relationship is supposed to be. So, we fabricate in our minds and our imagination what we romanticize about the most... the emotional aspect of 'feeling' good, safe, and with no problems. Well, no one romanticizes about heartaches and pains. We don't understand ourselves at a young age let alone being able to communicate with the opposite sex and comprehending our true needs.

Many unmet expectations lead to disappointments. Disappointments lead to us asking ourselves; 'what's wrong with me?' The 'what's wrong with me?' leads to anger, depression, abandonment, and defeat.

It's unfortunately how most girls lose their virginity before they feel ready and quite frankly don't know what to expect when they do engage in sexual intercourse for the first time.

Experiences from friends or other various media platforms become their 'guide' instead of the Bible guiding them. So, a young virgin girl having sex for the first time with a young boy who has had several sex partners before her, expects him to know what he's doing and how to protect her emotionally. Sadly, this is far from the truth.

The disappointment sets in and the "idea" of sex is formed. To have high expectations from someone who is unable to give or meet them is very discouraging. Abandonment is often felt due to the embarrassment, or the shame, or a false loyalty to each other due to the guilt. Unfortunately, this hurt is then passed on to the next relationship when the relationship does dissolve. The most important part of their life has now turned into a very traumatic experience.

Dysfunction and sinful behavior leads to a life of extremity, people-pleasing or control and manipulation. God's plans for us are good and prosperous, He didn't say dysfunctional and destructive. God does not want us to have or experience any of these things, but because of our choices, most do.

Even after Thomas and I remarried, I realized that I had unrealistic expectations of him and through attending marriage classes and talking things out, I was able to put those expectations into their proper place and out of our marriage.

His side:

We currently serve as Co-founders of As One Ministry, Inc., write marriage curriculum for churches, teach marriage workshops, conduct pre-marital coaching, officiate weddings together, and continue to grow and develop other husbands and wives through individual coaching.

I am more in love with my wife than ever before, we are growing in God together, and walking out the purpose He has for us individually as well as matrimonially. She is my best friend, confidant, lover and I place her second only to God.

If I were to share one thing with anyone having issues in their marriage, it would be to put God first, build your relationship with Him, then He can carry you through any valley you face. It is because of Him and the relationship we have that I can state He is the reason that what He put together, not even Natasha or I could tear apart. What I have learned is that God loves us unconditionally and if we are made in His image then we have to learn to forgive ourselves and others just like He forgives us.

I have not been perfect in my marriage to Natasha and she has called me to the floor on many aspects of my life. I have grown because of our relationship together and because of the relationship we have with God. If you are facing any issues in your life that are negatively affecting your marriage, confess it to God and then to your spouse. Learn to forgive one another and work at a solution that does not involve walking away from what God has put together.

After our remarriage to one another, we realized that God allowed us to experience a hurt so deep and be reconciled from it. We can now help others experience a resolution to the conflicts they are experiencing without the need for divorce.

2 Corinthians 1:3-4 ~ Blessed be God, even the Father of our Lord Jesus Christ, The Father of mercies, and the God of all comfort; Who comforteth us in all our tribulation, that we may be able to comfort them which are in any trouble, by the comfort wherewith we ourselves are comforted of God.

Only after the pain of divorce and walking out the process of forgiveness was God able to orchestrate the healing that was required to bring about restoration in our relationship.

Without yielding our hearts to His, we would not be able to share this gift from God through Holy Spirit. With all our hearts, we state that **it takes faith in the one who created us and His "Process of Forgiveness" to bring about healing in our marriage.** We believe He will do the same for you when you trust in Him.

Yes, it takes the act of humility, laying aside prideful behavior, and truly trusting the Lord as "**ALL things are possible to Him who believes." (Mark 9:23)**

PART II

BREAKING DOWN THE PROCESS

THE NEED FOR FORGIVENESS

You've read our story and you can see that forgiveness is a requirement if there is to be peace in the relationship between a husband and wife. The Bible informs us ***"But if ye forgive not men their trespasses, neither will your Father forgive your trespasses." ~ Matthew 6:16*** People often pray to God seeking forgiveness for things they have done but are holding on to unforgiveness where others are concerned. So, what is forgiveness? We like to define it as the action or process of pardoning the actions or words of or releasing negative feelings towards others. It does not mean that by doing so you are condoning or excusing the offense. Quite the opposite you are exposing the offense so acknowledgment of negative emotions can be relayed, and healing can begin.

"Forgiveness is a requirement if there is to be peace in the relationship of a husband and wife."

We may have a choice of whether we will forgive others or not. However, in God's eyes, holding on to unforgiveness is a sin. God wants to bless you according to His plans for you. Proverbs tells us that we should treat our enemies as though we care for them. ***"If thine enemy be hungry, give him bread to eat; and if he be thirsty, give him water to drink:" ~ Proverbs 25:21*** In this reference to the word enemy, the Hebrew word ***saw-nay*** is used. It means to hate, be hateful, an enemy. How much more should you be willing to resolve the issues in your marriage and create an atmosphere of peace in your household?

When you forgive, not only do you create an environment of peace in your home but your marriage as well. It can lead to a lifestyle of blessings if it's done the correct way. Imagine a life of blessings at every turn. Blessings that you expect from the works you do together and some that you don't expect because God Himself commands them. It takes most couples a while to figure out that when they determine to walk together, as one, God will be right there in the middle of it all. When we read the following scripture ***"Behold, how good and how pleasant it is for brethren to dwell together in unity! ...for there the LORD commanded the blessing, even life for evermore." ~ Psalm 133:1,3*** Imagine how good life would be when you and your spouse are working so much in tandem that God has to bless you because His word says so.

"You are exposing the offense so acknowledgment of hurt can be relayed, and healing begins."

FORGIVENESS HAS A PROCESS

We enjoy sharing the fact that we have a one hundred percent success rate when both husband and wife are on board with the process of forgiveness. ONE HUNDRED PERCENT! The process has little to do with us, it's all about the couple having a willing heart to trust Holy Spirit and the work He will do through us together. (Remember Psalm 133:1-3)

When we meet with couples, we take an assessment of their current situation according to their testimony to us. If a person leaves out a portion of the truth, the root cause of the problem takes longer to get to. An atmosphere of confidentiality and trust must be established in the beginning and confirmed before the start of the testimony, only then can the confidential nature of sharing and truthfulness take place.

Once confidentiality and trust are established the activity required for forgiveness is implemented. ***John 3:18 let us not love in word or in tongue, but in deed and in truth.*** Remember, forgiveness goes far beyond words. You may have experienced, a multitude of times, your spouse saying to you, "I'm sorry," or "I apologize," only to have the same issue take place days, weeks, or even months later. Why? Because forgiveness is a matter of the heart and is inclusive. To obtain true forgiveness, the emotions associated with the issue have to be addressed and God must be included.

When the statements, "I'm sorry!" and "I apologize" are used, it is a self-centered approach to problem resolution. Such statements do not include the offended person and do little to ensure that the same situation doesn't happen again.

"Forgiveness is a matter of the heart."

We choose to introduce the word "forgiveness" into the process because the word "forgive" is what you will find written in the Bible. If we are to pray the way Jesus tells us to pray, we should speak the language God has given us. The **Greek word for forgive is aphiemi (af-ee'-ay-mee). It means to send forth, to let go, to disregard**. So, the use of the word '**forgive**' when someone has wronged you, tends to weigh a little heavier than "**I'm sorry,**" which is placing a negative connotation on the offender. **I apologize** is mutually exclusive to the party that has been offended. The offender may be full of sorrow, however, they are not a sorry person. They are a child of God and are a great creation in Papa's eyes. **Understand why there can't be total healing when you utilize words that do not belong in the kingdom**. The kingdom of God is inclusive. Utilize words of the kingdom and you'll see things unfold before your eyes. The words you speak have life and death upon them. What are you speaking concerning your marriage and your spouse where conflict resolution is concerned?

The Bible tells us that the heart is the place of iniquity. We can change our minds about a person, place, or thing but true forgiveness happens when the heart is changed. We must also understand that a true change of heart happens only with the help of God. Consider Pharaoh during the exodus of the Israelites. Although Pharaoh committed to allowing the Israelites to leave Egypt, God decided that He would harden Pharaoh's heart for God's glory. ***"And I will harden Pharaoh's heart, and multiply my signs and my wonders in the land of Egypt. But Pharaoh shall not hearken unto you, that I may lay my hand upon Egypt, and bring forth mine armies, and my people the children of Israel, out of the land of Egypt by great judgments. And the Egyptians shall know that I am the LORD, when I stretch forth mine hand upon Egypt and bring out the children of Israel from among them." ~ Exodus 7:3-5*** It is always by a positive relationship with God that your heart is changed by Him and not by your own will.

What is essential is to not just believe what someone says to you but to read the source of information being presented. Having read the scripture, many will wonder why a loving God would treat a man in a position of leadership this way, or any man for that matter. We find our answer in Romans. ***"What if God, willing to shew his wrath, and to make his power known, endured with much longsuffering the vessels of wrath fitted to destruction: And that he might make known the riches of his glory on the vessels of mercy, which he had afore prepared unto glory, Even us, whom he hath called, not of the Jews only, but also of the Gentiles?" ~ Romans 9:22-24***

What we witness is that God is Sovereign and as the Creator of all things, He can and will do as He desires with what He created, to accomplish His objectives and goals. We learn that His actions are always in the best interest of those who have a good relationship with Him. Those who question Him must understand that God reserves the right to not only give us dominion, but He also holds others accountable for their actions concerning those whom He loves and has entrusted with his creation.

There is a key element in understanding the importance of forgiveness and it is found in Genesis when the statement is made, ***"God said, Let us make man in our image, after our likeness:" ~ Genesis 1:26*** Jesus was with God in the beginning and knew that the day would come when He would have to be manifest in human flesh, according to the will of the Father. His entire purpose was to bring forgiveness for the sins of mankind and bring us back into kingdom relationship with His Father.

When you understand the steps of identifying the conflict, it brings about the resolution of winning your spouse's heart back to you. During this process, it is key that you focus on having your spouse recall a specific time or place when identifying a conflict. This will help to ensure they are on board with the issue you want to discuss. This happens by following a pattern. We call this pattern the five "W's" and one "H." Six questions we encourage all couples to ask concerning each conflict they are contending with: Who, What, When, Where, Why, and How.

1. Determine WHO was involved.
2. Discuss WHAT the offense is.
3. Share WHEN the offense happened.
4. Discuss WHERE all parties were at the time of the offense.
5. Discuss HOW the offense came about.
6. Discuss WHY the offense happened.

When you learn to focus on these questions to bring about a resolution you will find that restoration and healing in your marriage will begin. Let's dive deeper into these questions by practical application.

Ready, let's go!

By using the following steps, you will be able to better identify the conflict.

TIMING

Knowing when to approach your spouse in regards to the conflict is just as important as your desire to want to resolve the matter.

- You must pray to God to ensure that your heart is in the right place and that you have the right motive for conflict resolution.
- Ensure that you are at peace before approaching your spouse so that you maintain an atmosphere of love within your relationship and your home. Approaching them when you are angry is not the best time to try to go through this process. "**Blessed**

are the peacemakers, for they will be called sons of God." (Matthew 5:9)

Practical Step:

A possible question

"Will you have time to talk later today/tonight as I'd like to share something that has been bothering me?"

HOW

Make sure that you have a good description of what happened. Record what was said or done to make you feel that you have been offended. Approaching your spouse with clarity about the offense will ensure only facts are shared.

Practical Step:

A suggested way to address your Spouse:

"When you said or did..."

WHO

Before you address the conflict with your spouse, you want to ensure that you have an understanding of the conflict yourself. Is it self-evident that your spouse is the one who caused the conflict? If the answer is yes, proceed. If no, spend more time in prayer and ask the Lord to search your heart according to **Philippians 4:6 – *"Be anxious for nothing but in everything by prayer and supplication, with thanksgiving, let your requests be made known to God."***

WHAT

Focus on identifying what was said or done to relay it to your spouse.

Practical Step:

Options for how to make the full statement:

"When you said you did not like the gift I bought you it made me feel hurt."

"When you threw the gift I gave you in the trash it really hurt me."

WHEN

It is important to bring your spouse to a moment in time when the conflict happened.

Practical Step:

A possible way to address when the offense took place:

"Last week, when you threw the gift, I gave you in the trash it made me feel really bad."

WHERE

The question of where is to further assist your spouse in recalling the situation.

Practical Step:

A possible way to address where the conflict took place:

"Last week, while we were at the restaurant and you threw the gift I gave you in the trash, it made me feel really bad."

WHY

The purpose of conflict resolution is to bring about unity so that God will continue to bless your marriage.

Practical Step:

A possible way to address why you want to resolve the conflict:

"I know that we have not spoken to each other in a few days because I have been upset. I want our marriage to move forward in unity. Last week, while we were at the restaurant and you threw the gift I gave you in the trash it made me feel really bad."

IDENTIFYING THE CONFLICT

A person's perception is their truth and often results in what is known as conflict.

Dictionary.com describes *conflict as a disagreement, to be contradictory, or in opposition.*

There's nothing wrong with disagreeing with someone. The questions are, have you been offended by the disagreement, and how are you going to resolve the conflict?

It's important during the process of any conflict resolution to maintain focus on the one conflict that is the subject matter at hand. Many marriages continue to suffer repetitive conflicts when becoming sidetracked by inserting other issues into the conversation. We call this moving the ***goal post***.

When the kicker on a football team is aiming for the field goal it is stabilized and does not move. In marriage, moving off-topic can cause more confusion in conflict resolution. Remember, to stay on the identified conflict topic the offended person (one who has been hurt) has asked to discuss and resolve.

Imagine a wall that is made of many bricks and you desire to get to the other side of that wall. You only have two tools, a chisel, and a hammer. How would you approach this situation? You would dismantle the wall by removing one brick at a time. The same goes for resolving marital conflict. Every issue in your marriage is a representation of a brick in the wall which has been built between you and your spouse. During the process of conflict resolution, you have to focus on one conflict or "brick" at a time.

The process of resolving conflict is tedious work but it is well worth it considering the vows that you made to your spouse, before God, and the witnesses to your wedding.

It is the job of the offended person (one who has been hurt) to approach the offender (one who caused the hurt) with the desire to resolve the conflict.

A person's perception is their truth

Perception is the organization, identification, and interpretation of sensory information in order to represent and understand the presented information or environment.

All perception involves signals that go through the nervous system, which in turn result from physical or chemical stimulation of the sensory system.

"Perception is reality" is an aphorism (concise, terse, laconic, or memorable expression of a general truth or principle) that is often used to justify a perception that may be objectively unjustifiable or out of touch with reality.

When understanding a person's perception, you must start the conversation from their point of view and hearing from their point of view. This is the story they are telling themselves and the objective is for them to share the specific hurt and not to generalize with statements such as "you always, you never, etc."; identify the hurt and express it clearly. It is not the Offended or the Offender's concern how the other will respond.

If you are **the Offended**, it's critical that you understand this **is your point of view** and it is up to you to convey from this stance. Do not assume or use general statements that are assumptive that everyone sees things as you do.

If you are **the Offender**, you must listen to what's being stated without defending yourself.

Acknowledge the who, what, when, and why of the conflict. The where is only important if the situation was brought about by a location that is not conducive to your relationship, such as a nightclub, concert, parent or friend's home, movie theater, etc. In the process of forgiveness, the **where** is best used when necessary to assist in the recall of the conflict that has taken place during the implementation of the resolution.

Example: "When I found out you were going to night clubs again without letting me know it made me feel..."

Answering who, what, and when will lead you to the how concerning the resolution. The how reveals the requirements in the establishment of boundaries for your relationship to assist with not having the conflict repeated in your marriage.

Example: "So that I don't make you feel... I will stop going to nightclubs completely because our marriage is worth it to me."

We highly recommend you utilize the Process of Forgiveness Worksheets at the end of this book to help guide you further through this process. You will be able to capture your thoughts in writing and use during your meeting with your spouse.

PRAY ABOUT THE CONFLICT

Before entering into a conversation concerning conflict, pray for yourself and your spouse. Doing so will ensure that God is included in the discussion. It also prepares your heart to receive, as well as give information in love.

The majority of the conflicts are caused by spiritual discord. **If you find that you have been contending with a conflict in your relationship with your spouse for some time, it is spiritual warfare.** Think about all the times that you both have said I forgive you, yet the same issue continues to happen. This could be reason to have concern that there is a deeper spiritual issue. Proverbs says, ***"Cast out the Scorner and contention shall go out; yea strife and reproach shall cease."*** ~ ***Proverbs 22:10*** The word scorn in the Hebrew language is pronounced "loots," it means to boast; to scorn; to deride; to talk arrogantly, or to be inflated. The characteristics of a scornful person are evidence that the person is full of pride.

"Before entering into a conversation concerning conflict pray for yourself and your spouse."

The Bible instructs us to cast out the scorner, in this case, it would be that spirit of pride that needs to be dealt with. **The scorner in your marriage is not your spouse it's not you either – it's that prideful spirit.** Pray that any pride you are contending with, would be overcome by Holy Spirit and that your spouse will forgive you as well.

PLAN A TIME FOR DISCUSSION

In consideration of Ecclesiastes, God lets us know that there is a time for all things. The following scripture is especially relevant regarding the process of forgiveness. " ***A time to rend, and a time to sew; a time to keep silence, and a time to speak;" ~ Ecclesiastes 3:7*** Your desire to address conflict may make matters worse if not addressed in God's timing. Planning your time and location for discussion is just as important as planning a family vacation. Before your departure, you make sure that your house is in order. When planning a discussion with your spouse concerning a conflict, you want to ensure that the environment in which the conversation is to take place is proper for the conversation. Also, you must examine your heart. **If your heart is not right, neither is the time.**

First, you want to let your spouse know that you want to have a conversation. Also, let him or her know how long you think the conversation may last and what it will be about. If you have children, you want to ensure that they do not cause interruptions. It's important to create an environment in which the two of you can share information without distractions. Because some conversations can become intense, you do not want to have a conversation in a public place such as a restaurant, family gathering, or when out with close friends.

It is important to remember that your conflict is between you, your spouse, and God. Ensure that you don't greet your spouse with the conflict as soon as they walk through the door. Give them time to unwind and relax, maybe eat dinner, and put the children to sleep, or drop them off with friends and family if possible.

The amount of time you spend setting the atmosphere before entering into the conversation will determine the level of success that you will have at the conclusion. It is important that you pray about the appropriate time for the discussion and ask God to soften your heart so that you can reach your spouse in a spirit of love.

The planning phase is the time you want to review the notes that you took concerning the conflict. Ensure that all of your questions and comments will be addressed in an orderly manner to bring about a positive result.

SETTING BOUNDARIES

When setting boundaries, it is very important the offender acknowledges the offense brought to their attention. The offender establishes the boundary (ies) and not generalize or give a blanket statement for all conflicts. Doing so allows for the offender to become aware that they are willing to care for the heart of the offended. It also allows Holy Spirit the opportunity to minister to the offender concerning the issue being discussed. We believe that no adult can change another adult, so the establishment of boundaries by the offender is key to self-exploration and self-control.

PART III

THE PROCESS OF FORGIVENESS

THE PROCESS

When discussing a conflict, it's important to remember that your ultimate goal is to find a resolution. What we've learned while marriage coaching is that there is a pattern conversations can have, that may be utilized to bring about positive results. It's important to not move the "goal post" or change the subject by adding an additional topic to the primary point of discussion. Doing so will only prolong the matter and may cause additional frustration between you and your spouse. This is the reason why it is so important to write the conflict during the identification step.

"When discussing a conflict, it's important to remember that your ultimate goal is to find a resolution."

When having your discussion, if you find that you've gotten off track there's nothing wrong with pausing the conversation, acknowledging the subject has changed, and returning to your main topic of discussion. There may be many other conflicts that go through your mind while you're discussing the primary conflict but keep in mind you resolve one conflict at a time in marriage because that's the way they usually happen.

If this is your first time tackling something major that you're contending with, start with something simple such as; leaving cabinet doors open, socks on the floor, sleeping with the television on, or maybe an impromptu honey-do list on your day off. While these topics may seem insignificant, if they are occurring, they can lead to much frustration over a period of time. Addressing minor infractions should be considered in the early stages of learning the process of forgiveness to ensure you are ready to implement it during the discussion about major marital conflicts.

Remember, before you begin to have your discussion about a minor issue, make sure you make time to pray with your spouse, asking Holy Spirit to guide you so your hearts are open to receive from one another and from the word of God. During this conversation, allocate time for you and your spouse to speak complete thoughts without interruption.

Also, if you are the Offender it is important to not defend yourself if your spouse shares with you that something you said or did caused them to have a negative emotional response. What that will sound like is, "When you said or did A, B, or C., it made me feel angry, hurt, abandoned, discouraged, alone, etc." **This is not the time for you to defend why you did or said what you did. It is time for you to intentionally hear the heart of your spouse.** Take a moment to reflect on Chapter 3 the fact that a person's perception is their truth. *(*See the Appendix at the end of this book for more emotional descriptors).*

THE POWER OF HONORING

When you were married you more than likely used the word honor during your marriage vows. Now is the time to truly implement that vow by honoring your spouse during this conversation. While you are having the discussion and those emotions are mentioned, you are to record them on a sheet of paper. Doing so will help ensure that you address each emotion in response to your spouse during the process of forgiveness. So if your spouse states that the causative nature of what you did or said made them feel displeased, unloved, neglected, alone etc, you will be able to address each component of their emotions by repeating to your spouse each emotion. This is a key part of intentional listening we call "mirror communication".

As the person who was offended, it's important to express every emotion that you experienced during the conflict. Again, you must take the time to write them down prior to your conversation with your spouse. Doing so will bring clarity to your conversation, eliminate frustrations and place the focus on yourself.

If you are the offender, your job at this point is to listen with your heart realizing that your spouse is the person who made a vow to honor, cherish, love, and be with you for the remainder of your time on earth. Record each emotional response that your spouse shares to ensure your spouse knows that you are listening intently. It also allows you to address everything they have shared from an emotional standpoint.

Defending yourself at this point means that you were trying to justify and/or fix the situation. Now is not the time to do so. The purpose of the process of forgiveness is to reconcile the differences and grow according to the principles found in the Bible. In the Gospel of Matthew when Peter went to Jesus and asked, ***"Then came Peter to him, and said, Lord, how oft shall my brother sin against me, and I forgive him? till seven times?" Jesus saith unto him, "I say not unto thee, Until seven times: but, Until seventy times seven."*** ~ ***Matthew 18: 21 -22*** What Jesus was sharing with Peter, and us as readers of the gospel, is that forgiveness is to be offered repeatedly. **However, if the conflicts are repetitive to the point of causing physical or mental abuse then you must protect yourself from a continuation of hurt and pain caused by your spouse.** Thus, there is not an indefinite number of times to forgive.

Know that with all the mercy and grace that is extended according to the words of Jesus to Peter, there was an endpoint. God does not want us to live life with a hardened heart caused by unforgiveness - thus the reason Moses made a decree of divorce. ***"He saith unto them, Moses because of the hardness of your hearts suffered you to put away your wives: but from the beginning it was not so."*** ~ **Matthew 19:8** Forgiveness is the way to soften your heart. If you choose to not forgive your spouse, you default to having a hardened heart – the path that leads to divorce.

The pattern of forgiveness was birthed through us by Holy Spirit as we reflected on what God did in us to reconcile our marriage. It is truly a delight to know that when we follow His lead, He gives us a pattern that will bring about a resolution in our times of need that leads to restoration.

For now, we want to focus on the process of forgiveness in your marriage to help you avoid the hardening of your heart.

First things first, before we dive into the actual steps of the process of forgiveness we must prepare. Much like getting ready to cook a new meal using a recipe, you should first gather your ingredients and organize them accordingly. It's the same with preparing to go into the process of forgiveness, you must ensure you are ready.

If you choose to not forgive your spouse, you default to having a hardened heart – the path that leads to divorce.

Let's define two words that are utilized within the process of forgiveness: Offended and Offender

Offended – The person who has been affected negatively by an action(s) or words by another.

Offender – The person who caused the negative emotions of another through action(s) or words.

1. **List of offenses.** For clarity and use during the conversation, make a list of the offenses and the individual emotions or feelings associated with each one. This will help you to stay on track and focused to ensure each offense has been addressed. (Utilize Worksheets at the end of this book)

2. **Pray to God** about the offense asking for wisdom and discernment about how and when to approach your spouse.

Be prepared to know that some offenses may not make it on your list because God will do a work in you first.

3. **Plan a time** to have a discussion with your spouse. Don't catch your spouse off guard with this process. It is important that you inform them of the meeting ahead of time. Doing so helps them to focus on their time with you.

4. **Pray together.** Before you begin the steps with your spouse, pray with your spouse about your hearts being open to receiving from one another with the understanding that you will resolve the conflict.

5. **Set a timer** if you know that either you, your spouse or both of you are long winded, we suggest you utilize a timer in the beginning until you have gone through this process a few times.

Now that we have the prep work done, it's time to dive in. Take a deep breath. Ready, let's go!

STOP – If your spouse has not read this book and is not in agreement with you concerning this process, we advise you to wait until he/she has read it and is in agreement to proceed.

STEP 1

MAKE THE CONFLICT KNOWN

Timing is of the essence to successfully address an offense and achieving a resolution that not only you and your spouse can be satisfied with, but one that now includes God and His desires for you and your spouse. Knowing when to approach a person concerning a conflict, will play a huge role in whether a resolution is found. It is important to ensure that the person has an idea of what they are being approached about and this is done by a statement as simple as, "I have something I would like to discuss with you concerning the kitchen when you have a moment." This type of approach works because **the opportunity for the offender to feel blind-sided is significantly reduced.** It also allows the offended person to create an atmosphere in which a resolution can be found by including the offender in the resolution. Remember, the reason for discussing the offense is to ensure the relationship can continue to grow and prosper.

Anytime an offended person addresses an offense, it should be done in love and not with ill intent. *"Moreover if thy brother shall trespass against thee, go and tell him his fault between thee and him alone: if he shall hear thee, thou hast gained thy brother."* ~ ***Matthew 18:15*** As Christians we should want to keep our family together and that means that we are to continuously desire to win the hearts of others.

"The reason for discussing the offense is to ensure the relationship can continue to grow and prosper."

Before discussing the offense with your spouse, you must pray to God together, including Him in the conversation, asking that His will be done concerning your marriage. *"Behold, how good and how pleasant it is for brethren to dwell together in unity! ...for there the LORD commanded the blessing – life forevermore."* ~ ***Psalm 133:1,3***

What we want to emphasize concerning these verses is **God's blessing is a commandment when you and your spouse are working at life and marriage together.** If you wonder why your marriage seems to struggle in certain areas, pray about it and bring it before your spouse and God to find a resolution.

When you are finished praying, position yourself so that you and your spouse can make eye contact, then get straight to the point of the conversation discussing only one topic – the offense. Now is not the time to defend yourself as the offender, nor is it the time for the offended to try and place guilt on the offender. God will defend you both if you trust the Holy Spirit to lead you through this work. After all, Holy Spirit is the healer.

We have experienced several sessions where a spouse (the offender) wanted to explain why they did or said something only to experience a rebuttal that moved the goal post or changed the subject to a degree that the process of forgiveness was delayed until we could get them back on track by reminding them to remain focused on one topic at a time. If this process is not managed well you will run the risk of creating more frustration, which leaves the enemy proclaiming victory against your marriage.

STEP 2

ACKNOWLEDGE THE OFFENSE AND ASK FOR FORGIVENESS

The offender has a particularly important role in the process of forgiveness. The role is not to defend anything you have said or done but to acknowledge the perception of the offense presented by the offended. It is important to remember that a person's perception is their truth. When the offender attempts to explain their position the offended becomes secondary to the issue that they are presenting. As a spouse, who is the offender, you want to ensure that you honor the voice and emotions that your spouse is presenting to you.

“A person's perception is their truth.”

At this point, the offender is to capture every negative emotion that your spouse is presenting by writing it down as it is presented. This is part of effective listening.

Once the offended has completed their statements, the offender has a perfect opportunity to begin to restore the marriage as found in the second half of a scripture in the book of **Matthew 18:15** ***"...if he shall hear thee, thou hast gained thy brother."*** As the offender, your role is to hear your spouse regardless of how you feel about the situation. It's their heart that you want to reconcile back to you. One of the things that I love about the church I attend is that my Pastor states: "If my wife is upset with me, I need to consider what I have done." This is a bold statement of humility in action. Consider that statement when your spouse approaches you. Was it something they stated you have done to offend them? **Humility in action is going through** the process of forgiveness **to resolve the conflict.**

"...for all have sinned and fall short of the glory of God," **Romans 3:23** ~ This scripture informs us that we all have missed the mark God desires for us to hit, which is different from making mistakes. Sin happens when we know the truth of a matter but choose not to follow God's word. A mistake happens when we misspell a word, or we forget to do something. The question to you is what have you believed, or what are you believing God for that you have not received? Could your unforgiveness play a role in the lack of the manifestation of what you're believing God for? When we choose not to forgive, we choose not to receive God's blessing because of the unforgiveness. ***"But if ye forgive not men their trespasses, neither will your Father forgive your trespasses."*** ~ **Matthew 6:15** When we begin to understand the correlation of forgiveness to the receiving of blessings we can move forward in a stronger ministry for our marriage and to our community.

Offering and receiving forgiveness is not about emotions, however requesting forgiveness is. When Jesus hung on the cross after being wrongfully accused, imprisoned, suffering an illegal trial, was beaten, forced to carry a cross, witnessing people who said they loved him only to abandon him, dishonored by his disciples, stripped naked, witnessed his clothes being sold, nailed to the cross, spat upon, having a crown of thorns from a rose bush placed upon his head, and all of this humiliation being done in front of his mother; offered words that set all of them free of what they had done.

"Then said Jesus, Father, forgive them; for they know not what they do." ~ Luke 23:34

As the offending spouse being approached by the offended spouse, the amount of peace in your marriage is weighed upon this principle - the principle of forgiveness. **From this point forward, in this one conversation, you carry the burden of removing one brick from the wall of separation between you and your spouse** and all you have to do is ask for forgiveness while acknowledging the emotions presented to you by your spouse.

If you will trust the pattern of forgiveness, you will enjoy and experience healing and freedom like you never have before. For those that refuse to go this route, we often find they are contending with a spirit of pride.

***"When pride cometh, then cometh shame: but with the lowly is wisdom." ~* Proverbs 11:2**

"The way of a fool is right in his own eyes: but he that hearkeneth unto counsel is wise." ~ Proverbs 12: 15

STEP 3

GRANT FORGIVENESS

You were made in the image of God and He is a forgiving God. He has already informed you that if you do not forgive, you will not be forgiven by Him.

Now is the time to search your heart and your soul and reflect on the vow that you made to your spouse when you were married. In the order of God's family, your spouse is the second most important person in your life after God. Remember Psalm 133 states where there is unity, God commands His blessings. Although forgiveness is a choice, where a Godly marriage is concerned the option should be clear. If you want a successful marriage, forgiveness is a founding principle when it is; recognized, discussed, and practiced according to Godly principles.

When offering forgiveness, it should be done with a sincere heart just as God is sincere and faithful when you ask Him for forgiveness with a heart of humility. When you offer forgiveness to your spouse you are operating in the image of God. God forgives you for anything you have done, except the blasphemy of Holy Spirit who was sent to comfort us.

"Verily I say unto you, All sins shall be forgiven unto the sons of men, and blasphemies wherewith soever they shall blaspheme: But he that shall blaspheme against the Holy Ghost hath never forgiveness, but is in danger of eternal damnation." ~ Mark 3:28-29

When your spouse approaches you with a sincere heart, led by Holy Spirit, and asks for forgiveness, it is not up to you to determine whether they need it or not. This is not the time to reflect on the emotions that you've already expressed. It's not the time to reflect on how the request for forgiveness is stated but to hear the words that are stated.

Look at your spouse and see them in the image of Jesus Christ who has covered all their sins already. Lay aside your hurt, anger, disappointments, and any other emotions or thoughts and trust Holy Spirit who is in you, because He has the power to change your spouse. **Now let your spouse know that you forgive them by looking them in their eyes while holding their hands and stating, "I forgive you."**

If you find this hard to do, consider **that forgiveness is an act of faith.** Not faith in your spouse, but faith that God will change the heart of your spouse through this process. ***"Now faith is the substance of things hoped for, the evidence of things not seen." ~ Hebrews 11:1*** If you are waiting on your heart to feel right about your spouse you have your faith misplaced. When we state that forgiving your spouse must come from your heart, we mean that your heart should be focused on your faith in God to do what you ask and help you guard your heart. As the offended person, your spouse, has nothing to do with you granting forgiveness. The unity that is spoken of in ~ **Psalm 133:1-4** and God's commanded blessing should be your motivation.

When we acknowledge our sins as a couple and implement the process of forgiveness, God hears our prayers and is faithful to heal our hearts.

"As the offended person your spouse has nothing to do with you granting forgiveness."

STEP 4

RECEIVE FORGIVENESS

The receiving of forgiveness is a simple step. At this moment, few words are needed but are particularly important in the healing process. The offended has extended forgiveness and as with any gift, not receiving it is likened to the blocking of a blessing. Forgiveness is a gift that comes from the heart and in this case, that heart belongs to your spouse.

An analogy that we like to use is that when the proposal of marriage was made, acceptance between a husband and a wife in the exchange of hearts took place. Each spouse agrees to allow the other to control the pulse of their heartbeat. When problems get escalated between the two it is usually because one or the other said or did something. Likewise, when things are comfortable, and life is flowing smoothly it is because someone said or did something. No one complains when things are going well.

The most important thing you can do at this point is to confirm the reunification of your hearts regarding the current conflict by saying, **"I receive your forgiveness."**

Doing so not only confirms that you have heard your spouse, but speaks life into your marriage and proves you have overcome the disunity the two of you previously walked in.

"And you shall know the truth, and the truth shall make you free." ~ John 8:32

STEP 5

PRAY

"In all thy ways acknowledge him, and he shall direct thy paths." ~ Proverbs 3:6

Merriam-Webster describes a problem as something that is difficult to deal with or something that is a source of trouble, worry, etc.

When you pray, both of you want to ensure that you acknowledge the problem. The following is a general truth or a piece of advice. God wants to be a part of your marriage and Proverbs 3:6 instructs us to acknowledge Him in all that we do; whether it's good or bad. **When we include Him in our discussions, He is faithful to help us.** Jesus, having been given all authority by God, allows us to use the same authority and power found in His name to resolve any conflict or problem. So, when you pray, it is important to utilize His name as you present yourselves before God.

As you pray with your spouse, **ask God to cover both of you concerning the conflict.** While you are praying, touch in agreement concerning the words you offer up. The bible encourages us to cast our cares onto the creator of all things. **Psalm 55:22** also informs us that He is faithful to sustain us when we do so. Remember that we are human and cannot forget what has happened to us, but we can trust God to place a hedge of protection around our marriage when we come into agreement with our spouse concerning any matter.

It is awesome to know that we have a God who is alive and who cares for us. That is why we are instructed by Peter, a disciple of Christ Jesus, in ***"Casting all your care upon him; for he careth for you." ~ 1 Peter 5:7***

When we choose to cast our cares to the Lord our God, we choose to free our spouse of the previous hurt that was caused. Some people say that you should forget those things that have hurt you. **It is human nature and God's design for us to remember what has hurt us so that we don't find ourselves repeating the same hurts**. Casting your cares simply means letting go of the hurt and pain that causes discord within your marriage. When you choose to revisit that hurt and pain, you elect to subject your spouse to unforgiveness once again. You also choose to tell God that He's not big enough to help you move through the hurt.

When we choose, as Christians, to operate outside of the word of God, we open the door to a proud nature. ***"A new heart also will I give you, and a new spirit will I put within you: and I will take away the stony heart out of your flesh, and I will give you an heart of flesh." ~ Ezekiel 36:26***

When we cast our cares onto God, we voluntarily allow Him to cause a change within us that is beneficial to our marriage. Doing so moves us into a place where we can create a testimony concerning the hurt we just overcame, in order to make disciples of others, by sharing how we overcame the problems in our marriage. Read the following verse and consider the underlined text: ***"Blessed be God, even the Father of our Lord Jesus Christ, the Father of mercies, and the God of all comfort; Who comforteth us in all our tribulation, that we may be able to comfort them which are in any trouble, by the comfort wherewith we ourselves are comforted of God. For as the sufferings of Christ abound in us, so our consolation also aboundeth by Christ."*** ~ ***2 Corinthians 1:3-5***

When we experience sufferings, it is to be used to grow our faith in God and for us to comfort others by sharing our testimony of how God got us through the pain. When we do so, we help others to get from under the bondages and heartaches that are so prevalent in marriages today. If you want a new heart, trust God with the pains that you will release through this marriage tool called, the process of forgiveness. Use it to tear down the wall containing each brick of conflict that has been placed between you and your spouse.

True forgiveness happens when you choose not to bring up past hurts that you have addressed through the process of forgiveness. You will have opportunities to bring the issue up in future conversations with your spouse because something will be said or done that will trigger the memory. It is important at this point that you guard not only your heart but the heart of your spouse. If you elect to bring up the past hurt, as a weapon, the entire process of forgiveness that you've gone through concerning an issue will be nothing more than a lie.

While it's important to acknowledge that you are still hurting because of emotions, it is also important to not hurt your spouse because of how you feel. You are in control of the destiny of your marriage. When you came into agreement to be married to one another, you gave your heart to your spouse. The pulse of your heart is determined by the level of peace in your marriage. Should you decide to bring up old hurts as a weapon against your spouse, you increase blood pressure, thereby shortening their lifespan. Choose to speak life to your spouse.

STEP 6

ESTABLISH BOUNDARIES

Boundaries are defined by Webster's Dictionary as, "something that indicates or fixes a limit or extent."

During your prayer time, you cast your prayer to God and hopefully prayed that you would not use the issue as a weapon against them in the future. Stating that during your prayer was the first step in establishing a spiritual boundary. Doing so in the spirit helps with doing so in the natural.

With every issue that you overcome, the two of you should establish boundaries to ensure that you do not fall back into the same issue again. There will be times that the thoughts and emotions will rise to the surface of your mind again and that is when it is time to implement ***Romans 12:2 ~ "And be not conformed to this world: but be ye transformed by the renewing of your mind, that ye may prove what is good, and acceptable, and perfect will of God."*** And ***2 Corinthians 10:5 ~ "Casting down imaginations, and every high thing that exalteth itself against the knowledge of God, and bringing into captivity every thought to the obedience of Christ."***

The healthiest part of healing a marriage is the establishment of boundaries. After you have completed the process of forgiveness, boundaries are established by capturing every thought that can lead to a stronghold of the spiritual enemy being re-established in your marriage. By doing so you will realize that over time the thought that could lead to returning to the bondage of anger, hurt, rejection, pain, etc will dissipate over time. ***James 4:7 ~ "Submit yourselves therefore to God. Resist the devil, and he will flee from you."***

It is important to note, the offender is the one to establish boundaries as they are stating what they will no longer do to cause those painful emotions to surface, again, associated with the offense brought to them.

Taking every thought captive is resisting the devil and just like the process of forgiveness, you will be responding according to God's word and not your will. ***Luke 11:21-22 - "When a strong man, fully armed, guards his own house, his possessions are safe. But when someone stronger attacks and overpowers him, he takes away the armor in which the man trusted and divides up the spoils."***

Verse 24 reminds us "When an evil spirit comes out of a man, it goes through arid places seeking rest and does not find it. Then it says "I will return to the house I left." When it arrives, it finds the house swept clean and put in order. Then it goes and takes seven other spirits more wicked than itself, and they go in and live there. And the final condition of that man is worse than the first."

It's imperative that the heart of man stays clean and washed of the word of God because if not, when you face that issue again, it will be worse than before; boundaries are your life vest for the rough waves but are safety nets for your spouse as well.

Proverbs 3:5-6 ~ "Trust in the LORD with all thine heart; and lean not unto thine own understanding. In all thy ways acknowledge him, and he shall direct thy paths."

2 Corinthians 5:17 ~ "Therefore if anyone is in Christ, he is a new creation. The old has passed away. Behold, the new has come."

Rinse and Repeat

CONGRATULATIONS! You have completed a full round of addressing one conflict. Now, you are ready to move to the next conflict in your list. Remember to stay on one topic at a time and do not move the goal post. Hopefully, your spouse is also partaking in the process of forgiveness and if so, after you share one topic from your list, allow them to share a topic and you both alternate until you have completed all items of contention on your lists.

Ideally, you won't get through both lists in one day so we recommend that you set aside 1 day a week for 2 hours for the next 3 weeks and be intentional about going through the process of forgiveness. Do this for the next 3 weeks you will see the difference in how you choose to handle conflict and don't be surprised if you are witness to a 'new thing' in your marriage.

USE THE CONFLICT AS A TOOL FOR MINISTRY

"The thing that hath been, it is that which shall be; and that which is done is that which shall be done: and there is no new thing under the sun." ~ Ecclesiastes 1:9

You are not alone in what you are experiencing in your marriage. The reason you struggle with different conflicts is that no one has shared their testimony of how they have overcome it, to the extent that you could apply their processes to your marriage. You have now been given a process to not only resolve your conflict but to share with others the Godly principles that have been shared with you.

When you go through trials of life and marriage, it is almost inevitable that someone will come along who is experiencing the same issue. If you have been blessed by God to have overcome conflict in your marriage, as a Christian, it is your duty to share how you did it so that you might create disciples through your marital experience.

"You have now been given a process to not only resolve your conflict but to share with others the Godly

principles that have been shared with you."

Let your marriage be a light to others because people are hurting and desiring wisdom and understanding. Will you share your new-found freedom with them as we have with you?

CONCLUSION

Did you know that most cancerous cells thrive because of a lack of oxygen delivered to the body? When cancer is exposed to oxygen it dies. God is asking you to allow His breath of life to enter into the cancerous areas of your relationship through His word while you learn The Process of Forgiveness. When the problems of your marriage are addressed through unity, in agape love, a successful marriage is commanded according to **Psalm 133:1-3** ***"Behold, how good and how pleasant it is for brethren to dwell together in unity! It is like the precious ointment upon the head, that ran down upon the beard, even Aaron's beard: that went down to the skirts of his garments; As the dew of Hermon, and as the dew that descended upon the mountains of Zion: for there the*** LORD ***commanded the blessing, even life for evermore."***

There comes a time in everyone's life when we realize that the "elephant in the room" didn't just show up. That elephant represents a lot of small things that were never properly addressed for the sake of not causing friction in your relationship. Remember that the small, unaddressed situations become so ingrained in a strand of negativity that if it continues to be left alone it ends up like cancer.

This is how we overcome the adversary. **This is how we stay together. Forgiving daily and often.** Remember one of the questions we are asked is, "How do we stay together?" This is it. **The Process of Forgiveness is our glue – forgiveness with the intention of sharing agape love.**

It is the goal of 'As One Ministry' to empower couples with tools for a successful marriage. We work to help you experience a marriage of peace, true love, worship of God, and to set you on a path of making disciples through your marital lifestyle. You are being watched, whether by your children, coworkers, friends, or family. How is your marriage being a testimonial for others?

The process of forgiveness is a tool for you to implement in your relationship with your spouse first, so that your household can be made whole as you teach it to your children and second, to extended family and community.

Be blessed as you incorporate this Process of Forgiveness into the DNA of your marriage.

COUPLE TESTIMONIAL

MELVIN AND PATRICIA ARPS

Melvin:

Patricia and I met Thomas and Natasha Gibson through a marriage class at our church in the Dallas, Fort Worth, TX Metroplex. They were our group facilitators and we really liked their energy and enthusiasm for the Lord. However, we did not get to know them really until later in our marriage when we would call upon their marriage coaching services. Trish and I have been married for 5 years and the first two years were really rough for us as we met and married 7 months after meeting. When we married, we really did not know each other but we started learning more about each other rather quickly, post-marriage. We realized how different we were and how much alike we were and the differences were causing us to have a lot of friction in our relationship.

We sought help and tried Christian counselors, but they did not sit well with me as I felt they were concentrating more on me, as the problem. We then went through the marriage curriculum program via our church and it helped quite a bit with our communication issues and provided great practical communication tools. However, we were still having some challenges and decided we would try private mentoring. We reached out to try Thomas and Natasha's marriage principles through As One Ministry. They were effective. They provided us with individual mentoring which was highly effective in helping me to take an inward view of myself. Trish told me several times she believed I had father issues. I did not believe I did and vehemently denied I did. I was in a mentoring session with Thomas and he asked me if I felt I had father issues. I replied that I did not. He listened as I denied these issues and we continued talking. A little while later he asked what I felt the issues were with me. I told him I did not like to be controlled. He then asked where do you think that comes from? I replied, "My father was controlling" and I stopped and looked at him and said "you think you are slick!" We laughed but I realized that maybe Trish was right. Thomas and Natasha gave us tools and helped us realize who we are to ourselves and one another.

Trish:

From my perspective, I looked forward to the opportunity of meeting someone that I could love and could love me eternally. I found that in Melvin. However, my challenges came from unrealized expectations. I had been married twice before and experienced great heartbreak and became a bit disillusioned regarding marriage. I went through singles counseling, divorce-care, and individual self-development programs in order to work on me. Then 3 ½ years later, I met Melvin. He was funny and full of conversation. He pursued my heart and wanted to get to know me. Though I was reluctant at first, I eventually softened. Melvin wasted no time asking me to marry him. I had dated a few people after my second marriage, but quickly decided against a future with either of them. Melvin seemed different, so I gave him a chance. Within 7 months we were married. After marriage, I wanted to continue to hang out and have fun, sit, and talk, and be romantic. Melvin did not see these characteristics as part of a marriage. He wanted to have "quality time, alone". (In which there is nothing wrong with this version of "quality time" as this had been his norm and to this day, I still give him that space, as he enjoys being able to zone out and be in his world) it's just that I have never associated "quality time" as an alone process.

This is where communication, understanding and growth needed to occur. Not having these characteristics in our marriage was a deal-breaker to me. As I wanted the touch, the time, and the talk. However, having too much of the intense time together was overwhelming for Melvin. I found it difficult to convey my feelings and frustrations to Melvin, because to him I was expressing personal dissatisfaction of who he was as a person. And to me, not talking about the issues was a personal rejection of who I was as a person.

I knew that I loved him and that he loved me, but we had this barrier of communication that kept us from getting to the heart issues. Thomas provided individual mentoring to Melvin and invited me to reach out to Natasha as an option, which I did on a few occasions. Melvin and I began to benefit from the insight and wisdom of Thomas and Natasha and made a commitment to The Process of Forgiveness and communication, two of the cornerstones of As One Ministry.

It was through this ministry that Melvin and I turned the corner and began to make God the focus of our marriage and sincerely worked on the process. God used many tools to help us to arrive to a point where we could turn to Him, turn to his Word, and to Prayer for us to see the fruit begin to blossom. Melvin and I had to learn that the both of us would need to give each other the best of us to see the fruit in us blossom. The best of us was making God the center of our home through using his Word and Prayer as the main ingredient in our marriage.

Melvin:

Married life has become so much better for us. Patricia is a part of Natasha's women's prayer group "Wives of Power" and I am one of the prayer leaders under Thomas' men's prayer group called "Kingdom Husbands". Trish and I lead a small group for married couples, and we continue to invest in our marriage through date nights, using the tools we have acquired, and gaining new marriage insight through obtaining various marriage materials and attending marriage conferences. Thomas and Natasha are always there whenever we need someone to talk to and/or confide in. We treasure their ministry and friendship.

PART IV

WORKSHEETS

WORKSHEETS

THE PROCESS OF FORGIVENESS

The following worksheets are designed to get you started by helping you to identify a conflict and resolving it through the 6-Step process of forgiveness.

It is important to ensure that you are in the mindset of finding a resolution when addressing each point of contention. Praying before you meet with your spouse sets the tone of peace and invites the presence of God into the situation prior to having a conversation with your spouse. Pray first, then begin.

NOTE: To expound beyond these pages, we also suggest that you create a separate list of contentions and take each one of them through the 6-Step Process of Forgiveness. If you find that you are having difficulties in resolving conflict contact us at contact@asoneministry.net and we will arrange marriage coaching sessions with you and your spouse.

The Offended:

The person who is experiencing the unhealthy emotions caused by the actions of another. Action required for Steps 1, 3, and 5.

*Refer to the Appendix for a list of emotions to express

The Offender:

The person whose actions, behaviors, or words has caused another person to experience unhealthy emotions.

Action required for Steps 2, 4, 5, and 6.

Lead:

The person who starts the process in each step.

Scriptures are given as a point of reference as the foundation for each step. Read and reflect on the scripture to help you understand that particular step within the process. Remember, you are completing these steps by faith and casting all cares and anxieties to the Lord.

Example Statements are given to show you the outcome of the step you are working toward to complete that step. Writing down your thoughts and statement before the meeting will help you to stay on track and not move the goal post.

Summary of 6-Step Process of Forgiveness

Step 1: Make the Conflict Known

Supporting Scripture:

Matthew 18:15

Step 2: Acknowledge the Offense & Ask for Forgiveness

Supporting Scripture:

Matthew 6:14-15

Step 3: Grant Forgiveness

Supporting Scriptures:

John 8:32, Matthew 6:14-15

Step 4: Receive Forgiveness

Supporting Scripture:

1 Peter 5:7

Step 5: Pray Together

Supporting Scriptures:

James 5:13-16, Psalm 133:1-3

How to pray - Matthew 6:5-13,

Step 6: Set Boundaries

Supporting Scriptures:

Luke 11:24-26, Proverbs 4:23-27

WORKSHEET STEP 1 – MAKE THE CONFLICT KNOWN

LEAD: THE OFFENDED

Purpose:

To capture your thoughts and the emotions around the offense.

Scripture:

"Moreover if thy brother shall trespass against thee, go and tell him his fault between thee and him alone: if he shall hear thee, thou hast gained thy brother."

~ ***Matthew 18:15***

Example Statement:

*"John, when we were at your mother's house last week and you made the comment to your mom that I should've worn the other dress, **it made me feel hurt, disrespected, isolated, and confused."***

What is your Conflict:

When we were at John's mother's house last week, he made a comment about my dress

What are the emotions around the Conflict:

Hurt, disrespected, isolated, and confused

Statement to be given:

John, when we were at your mother's house last week, you said my dress was ugly and it made me feel hurt, disrespected, isolated, and confused.

WORKSHEET STEP 2 - ACKNOWLEDGE THE OFFENSE AND ASK FOR FORGIVENESS

LEAD: THE OFFENDER

Purpose:

To capture the emotions stated by the Offended and consider if it was your intent to cause the offense and ask for forgiveness.

Scripture:

For if ye forgive men their trespasses, your heavenly Father will also forgive you: But if ye forgive not men their trespasses, neither will your Father forgive your trespasses.

~ ***Matthew 6:14-15***

Example Statement:

"Jane, when I made the comment to my mother about your dress, it was not my intention to make you feel hurt, disrespected, isolated, and confused. ***Will you forgive me?"***

What is the offense:

What are the emotions stated:

Make your statement:

What additional thoughts around this offense come to mind? You may realize you stated what you did because of a past issue (capture the thought(s) by writing it here and note you will address these when you are in the offended role after your spouse's issue is addressed).

WORKSHEET STEP 3 – GRANT FORGIVENESS

LEAD: THE OFFENDED

Purpose:

Your response at this time is to simply grant forgiveness based on the offender's request.

Scripture:

"And ye shall know the truth, and the truth shall make you free."

~ John 8:32

"For if ye forgive men their trespasses, your heavenly Father will also forgive you: But if ye forgive not men their trespasses, neither will your Father forgive your trespasses."

~ Matthew 6:14-15

Example Statement:

"Yes, I forgive you."

If you are hesitant to grant forgiveness, capture your thoughts as to why:

Continue to be in prayer about your hesitations and respond by faith; not by your perception if the offender is sincere or not.

WORKSHEET STEP 4 – RECEIVE FORGIVENESS

LEAD: THE OFFENDER

Purpose:

Your response at this time is to simply receive the forgiveness.

Scripture:

Casting all your care upon him; for he careth for you.

~ 1 Peter 5:7

Example Statement:

"I receive your forgiveness"

If you are hesitant to receiving forgiveness, capture your thoughts as to why:

Continue to be in prayer about your hesitations and respond by faith; not by your perception that the offended believes you or not.

WORKSHEET STEP 5 – PRAY

LEAD: THE OFFENDER

Purpose:

Your response at this time is to pray with the offended and asking God for His forgiveness for causing the emotions expressed and continue with how Holy Spirit leads you to pray.

Scripture:

"Is any among you afflicted? Let him pray. Is any merry? Let him sing psalms. Is any sick among you? Let him call for the elders of the church; and let them pray over him, anointing him with oil in the name of the Lord: And the prayer of faith shall save the sick, and the Lord shall raise him up; and if he have committed sins, they shall be forgiven him. Confess your faults one to another, and pray one for another, that ye may be healed. The effectual fervent prayer of a righteous man availeth much."

~ James 5:13-16

"A Song of degrees of David. Behold, how good and how pleasant it is for brethren to dwell together in unity! It is like the precious ointment upon the head, that ran down upon the beard, even Aaron's beard; that went down to the skirts of his garments; As the dew of Hermon, and as the dew that descended upon the mountains of Zion; for there the LORD commanded the blessing, even life for evermore.

~ ***Psalms 133***

"When ye pray, say, Our Father which art in heaven, Hallowed be thy name. Thy kingdom come. Thy will be done, as in heaven, so in earth.

~ **Luke 11:2**

"And when thou prayest, thou shalt not be as the hypocrites are: for they love to pray standing in the synagogues and in the corners of the streets, that they may be seen of men. Verily I say unto you, They have their reward. But thou, when thou prayest, enter into thy closet, and when thou hast shut thy door, pray to thy Father which is in secret; and thy Father which seeth in secret shall reward thee openly. But when ye pray, use not vain repetitions, as the heathen do: for they think that they shall be heard for their much speaking. Be not ye therefore like unto them: for your Father knoweth what things ye have need of, before ye ask him. After this manner therefore pray ye: Our Father which art in heaven, Hallowed be thy name. Thy kingdom come, Thy will be done in earth, as it is in heaven. Give us this day our daily bread. And forgive us our debts, as we forgive our debtors. And lead us not into temptation, but deliver us from evil: For thine is the kingdom, and the power, and the glory, for ever. Amen.

~ ***Matthew 6:5-13***

Example Statement:

"Let's Pray"

Note: If the offended has something to pray concerning this topic, they may do so after your prayer.

WORKSHEET STEP 6 – ESTABLISH BOUNDARIES

LEAD: THE OFFENDER

Purpose:

Your response at this time is to set boundaries that will help you to not give rise to those negative emotions the offended person has brought to your attention through this process. It is important that YOU establish the boundaries and not the person who is offended. Holy Spirit will put you in remembrance of what you confess with your mouth.

Scripture:

"When the unclean spirit is gone out of a man, he walketh through dry places, seeking rest; and finding none, he saith, I will return unto my house whence I came out. And when he cometh, he findeth it swept and garnished. Then goeth he, and taketh to him seven other spirits more wicked than himself; and they enter in, and dwell there: and the last state of that man is worse than the first.

~ Luke 11:24-26

"Keep thy heart with all diligence; for out of it are the issues of life. Put away from thee a forward mouth, and perverse lips put far from thee. Let thine eyes look right on, and let thine eyelids look straight before thee. Ponder the path of thy feet, and let all thy ways be established. Turn not to the right hand nor to the left: remove thy foot from evil.

~ ***Proverbs 4:23-27***

Example Statement:

"Jane, I will no longer make comments outside of our marriage about your attire. If I have an issue with what you are wearing, I will have that discussion with you because I do not want to make you feel hurt, disrespected, isolated, and confused again."

What are the boundaries:

NOTES

APPENDIX

EMOTIONAL DESCRIPTORS

Abandoned
Agonizing
Alienated
Anger
Anxious
Apathetic
Ashamed
Awful
Broken
Confused
Crushed
Depressed
Detestable
Devastated
Disappointed
Discredited
Disgruntled
Disillusioned
Dismayed
Disparaged
Disrespected
Distant
Distressed
Embarrassed
Empty
Enraged
Frightened
Frustrated
Furious
Guilty
Hateful
Hesitant
Hostile
Humiliated
Hurt
Ignored
Inadequate
Indifferent
Inferior
Infuriated
Insecure
Insignificant
Irritated
Isolated
Jealous
Judgmental
Lied To
Lonely
Mad
Overwhelmed
Pain
Perplexed
Powerless
Provocative
Provoked
Rejected
Remorseful
Repugnant
Resentful
Ridiculed
Sad
Sarcastic
Scared
Skeptical
Startled
Submissive
Suspicious
Terrified
Threatened
Victimized
Vulnerable
Withdrawn
Worried
Worthless

BIBLICAL REFERENCES (NKJV)

"Behold, I will do a new thing; now it shall spring forth; shall ye not know it? I will even make a way in the wilderness, and rivers in the desert."

~ ***Isaiah 43:19***

"So shall my word be that goeth forth out of my mouth: it shall not return unto me void, but it shall accomplish that which I please, and it shall prosper in the thing whereto I sent it."

~ ***Isaiah 55:11***

"Can two walk together, except they be agreed?" ~ ***Amos 3:3***

"But if ye forgive not men their trespasses, neither will your Father forgive your trespasses.

~ ***Matthew 6:16***

"If thine enemy be hungry, give him bread to eat; and if he be thirsty, give him water to drink:"

~ ***Proverbs 25:21***

"Behold, how good and how pleasant it is for brethren to dwell together in unity! ...for there the LORD commanded the blessing, even life for evermore."

~ ***Psalm 133:1,3***

"And I will harden Pharaoh's heart, and multiply my signs and my wonders in the land of Egypt. But Pharaoh shall not hearken unto you, that I may lay my hand upon Egypt, and bring forth mine armies, and my people the children of Israel, out of the land of Egypt by great judgments. And the Egyptians shall know that I am the LORD, *when I stretch forth mine hand upon Egypt, and bring out the children of Israel from among them."*

~ ***Exodus 7:3-5***

"What if God, willing to shew his wrath, and to make his power known, endured with much longsuffering the vessels of wrath fitted to destruction: And that he might make known the riches of his glory on the vessels of mercy, which he had afore prepared unto glory, Even us, whom he hath called, not of the Jews only, but also of the Gentiles?"

~ ***Romans 9:22-24***

"God said, Let us make man in our image, after our likeness:"

~ ***Genesis 1:26***

"Moreover if thy brother shall trespass against thee, go and tell him his fault between thee and him alone: if he shall hear thee, thou hast gained thy brother."

~ ***Matthew 18:15***

"And he said unto them, Go ye into all the world, and preach the gospel to every creature."

~ ***Mark 16:15***

"Cast out the Scorner and contention shall go out; yea strife and reproach shall cease."

~ ***Proverbs 22:10***

" A time to rend, and a time to sew; a time to keep silence, and a time to speak;"

~ ***Ecclesiastes 3:7***

" Then came Peter to him, and said, Lord, how oft shall my brother sin against me, and I forgive him? till seven times?" Jesus saith unto him, "I say not unto thee, Until seven times: but, Until seventy times seven."

~ ***Matthew 18: 21-22***

"He saith unto them, Moses because of the hardness of your hearts suffered you to put away your wives: but from the beginning it was not so."

~ **Matthew 19:8**

"Moreover if thy brother shall trespass against thee, go and tell him his fault between thee and him alone: if he shall hear thee, thou hast gained thy brother."

~ ***Matthew 18:15***

"Behold, how good and how pleasant it is for brethren to dwell together in unity! ...for there the LORD commanded the blessing – life forevermore."

~ ***Psalm 133:1,3***

"if he shall hear thee, thou hast gained thy brother."

~ **Matthew 18:15**

"for all have sinned and fall short of the glory of God,"

~ **Romans 3:23**

"But if ye forgive not men their trespasses, neither will your Father forgive your trespasses."

~ **Matthew 6:15**

"Then said Jesus, Father, forgive them; for they know not what they do."

~ ***Luke 23:34***

"When pride cometh, then cometh shame: but with the lowly is wisdom."

~ **Proverbs 11:2**

"The way of a fool is right in his own eyes: but he that hearkeneth unto counsel is wise."

~ **Proverbs 12: 15**

"Verily I say unto you, All sins shall be forgiven unto the sons of men, and blasphemies wherewith soever they shall blaspheme: But he that shall blaspheme against the Holy Ghost hath never forgiveness, but is in danger of eternal damnation."

~ ***Mark 3:28-29***

"Now faith is the substance of things hoped for, the evidence of things not seen."

~ Hebrews 11:1

"In all thy ways acknowledge him, and he shall direct thy paths."

~ Proverbs 3:6

"Casting all your care upon him; for he careth for you."

~ 1 Peter 5:7

"A new heart also will I give you, and a new spirit will I put within you: and I will take away the stony heart out of your flesh, and I will give you an heart of flesh."

~ Ezekiel 36:26

"Blessed be God, even the Father of our Lord Jesus Christ, the Father of mercies, and the God of all comfort; Who comforteth us in all our tribulation, that we may be able to comfort them which are in any trouble, by the comfort wherewith we ourselves are comforted of God. For as the sufferings of Christ abound in us, so our consolation also aboundeth by Christ."

~ 2 Corinthians 1:3-5

"The thing that hath been, it is that which shall be; and that which is done is that which shall be done: and there is no new thing under the sun."

~ Ecclesiastes 1:9

"Behold, how good and how pleasant it is for brethren to dwell together in unity! It is like the precious ointment upon the head, that ran down upon the beard, even Aaron's beard: that went down to the skirts of his garments; As the dew of Hermon, and as the dew that descended upon the mountains of Zion: for there the LORD *commanded the blessing, even life for evermore."*

~ ***Psalm 133:1-3***

OTHER REFERENCES

2019 American Community Survey:

https://www.census.gov/programs-surveys/acs

ABOUT THE AUTHORS

Thomas & Natasha Gibson

Being a native Texan and North Carolinian, their paths crossed in Texas while working at the same company. Thomas and Natasha Gibson are Co-Founders of As One Ministry, Inc. as Marriage Ambassadors for Christ. As One Ministry, Inc. is an organization founded on biblical principles with a focus on family life and emphasis on empowering couples with tools for a successful marriage. Both are licensed ministers, Certified SYMBIS Facilitators, and Natasha is a Certified Life Coach.

Their ministry services include pre-marital and marital coaching, and by the leading of the Holy Spirit, will continue to coach others through their difficult times. In addition to doing the work with the ministry, Thomas is a successful residential Realtor® and Natasha is CEO of NG Consultants, Inc., a virtual administration and life coaching organization for entrepreneurs and a virtual executive administration training organization.

They have been married for 19 years and know the trials and difficulties life has to offer. Having experienced divorce from one another, they now rejoice in the restoration of their marriage and are excited about sharing their experience and helping other couples through their turbulent times.

The Gibsons are a blended family with three adult children and two grandsons. Both enjoy road trips together and their most memorable trip was to the Texas Hill Country, where they now call home.

Contact Information:

Email | contact@asoneministry.net

Website |www.asoneministry.net

Instagram | instagram.com/asoneministry1

COUPLES COACHING SERVICES

As One Ministry

Empowering couples with tools for a successful marriage.

www.AsOneMinistry.net

As One Ministry utilizes the Holy Bible, coaching skills, SYMBIS Assessment, and the Process of Forgiveness coaching methodology to empower individuals and couples to resolve current issues. We are not licensed counselors, therapists, attorneys, or psychologists. We also do not provide therapy or legal advice.

As One Ministry coaching team will coach you with tangible and non-tangible tools designed to improve your skills to solve problems and create spiritual development, however the results of the use of these tools are determined by your commitment to the coaching provided.

Our services include Pre-marital, Marital, and Individual coaching. We also offer various events and other developmental platforms such as workshops, and weekly prayer calls. If you are interested in any of these services, you may go directly to our website for our current contact information, updated events and educational platforms.

FUTURE PUBLICATIONS FROM AS ONE MINISTRY

The Process of Forgiveness Series:

1. The Process of Forgiveness - the effect in Marriage
2. The Process of Forgiveness - the effect in Parenting
3. The Process of Forgiveness - the effect in Leadership

Coming soon...

- P.S. I Didn't Always Love You
- A Journey Home; Awaken the Sleeping Giant
- The Apologetics of Politics

DIVINE FLOW PUBLISHING

Publishing People of Influence

onto Platforms for Impact.

The Lord gives the word [of power];

the women who bear and publish [the news]

are a great host. Psalm 68:11 AMPC

www.DivineFlowPublishing.com

CHARITY - CHAT N CHEW

Chat n' Chew

RESTORE, RECLAIM & REJOICE

Who Are We?

Chat-n-Chew was created in 2017.
We are a faith-based 501(c)(3) organization operated solely by volunteers. We do not have any paid staff.
We support displaced single-parents who left an abusive relationship and/or are experiencing homelessness due to trials and hardships beyond their control. We assist with household items, clothing, food/groceries, and assistance in locating suitable shelter.

Our Goal is to **RESTORE** self-sustainability,
RECLAIM self-confidence, and
REJOICE with our single parent heroes!
As they heal and emerge from the remnants of their past. We offer mentoring, coaching and prayer partners should an individual choose to participate.
Our Vision is to have a transitional home community called Streams of Water for homeless single parents.
https://www.chatnchew.org/

Made in the USA
Columbia, SC
14 March 2021

34275937R00085